D1302454

jB KEN
Harper, Judith E., 1953-
John F. Kennedy : our
thirty-fifth president
1567668690

C.2

OCT 0 6 2004

JOHN F. *Kennedy*

STORRS LIBRARY
693 Longmeadow Street
Longmeadow, MA 01106

DISCARD

Our PRESIDENTS

JOHN F. *Kennedy*

OUR THIRTY-FIFTH PRESIDENT

By Judith E. Harper

SPIRIT
of America®

The Child's World®
Chanhassen, Minnesota

9

JOHN F. *Kennedy*

Published in the United States of America by The Child's World®
PO Box 326 • Chanhassen, MN 55317-0326 • 800-599-READ • www.childsworld.com

Acknowledgments

The Creative Spark: Mary Francis-DeMarois, Project Director; Elizabeth Sirimarco Budd, Series Editor; Robert Court, Design and Art Direction; Janine Graham, Page Layout; Jennifer Moyers, Production

The Child's World®: Mary Berendes, Publishing Director; Red Line Editorial, Fact Research; Cindy Klingel, Curriculum Advisor; Robert Noyed, Historical Advisor

Photos

Cover: portrait of John F. Kennedy by Jamie Wyeth, reproduced with permission from the artist. Archive Photos/Deutsche Presse Agentur: 29; CORBIS: 36, 37; David M. Budd Photography, 7; John Fitzgerald Kennedy Library, Boston, MA: 6, 9, 10 (courtesy of Dorothy Wilding), 12, 13, 14 (©Fabian Bachrach), 15, 17, 19, 20 (©Toni Frissell, Library of Congress), 21, 22, 23, 27, 28, 30, 31, 34, 35; Library of Congress: 25; National Aeronautics and Space Administration (NASA): 32

Registration

The Child's World®, Spirit of America®, and their associated logos are the sole property and registered trademarks of The Child's World®.

Copyright © 2002 by The Child's World®. All rights reserved. No part of this book may be reproduced or utilized in any form or by any means without written permission from the publisher.

Library of Congress Cataloging-in-Publication Data

✓ Harper, Judith E., 1953–
  ✓ John F. Kennedy : our thirty-fifth president / by Judith E. Harper.
      p. cm.
    Includes bibliographical references (p.) and index.
  ✓ ISBN 1-56766-869-0 (library bound : alk. paper)
    1. Kennedy, John F. (John Fitzgerald), 1917–1963—Juvenile literature. 2. Presidents—United States—Biography—Juvenile literature. [1. Kennedy, John F. (John Fitzgerald), 1917–1963.
  2. Presidents.] I. Title.
    E842.Z9 H25 2001
    973.922'092—dc21

                                  2001000300

13   23   36

Contents

Chapter ONE	A Bright Future	6
Chapter TWO	High Hopes: The Young Politician	14
Chapter THREE	The Crisis Years	22
Chapter FOUR	Triumph and Tragedy	30
	Time Line	38
	Glossary Terms	40
	Our Presidents	42
	Presidential Facts	46
	For Further Information	47
	Index	48

A Bright Future

At age 43, John F. Kennedy was the youngest man ever elected president. He was also the first president born in the 20th century.

IT WAS NOVEMBER 9, 1960, THE DAY AFTER Election Day. At about nine in the morning, John F. Kennedy learned that he had been elected president of the United States. The total electoral vote showed that he defeated Vice President Richard Nixon by 303 to 219. It is the electoral vote that determines who will be president, not the ballots of American voters. The electoral vote includes all the votes cast by the members of the electoral college in each state.

It took weeks for the popular vote—the votes of the American people—to be counted and recounted. Kennedy was stunned to learn that his victory was extremely small. Out of more than 68 million votes cast, he received only 118,500 more than Nixon.

Kennedy received 49.7% of the popular vote, and Nixon earned 49.6%. In terms of the people's vote, it was the closest presidential race of the 20th century.

Kennedy's family was jubilant about his triumph, but he was worried. He had been sure of a larger victory. Yet nearly half of all voters did not choose him to be president. As Kennedy saw it, a huge challenge stood before him. He would have to prove to the American

John F. Kennedy was born in this six-room, two-story house in Brookline, Massachusetts, a busy town nestled next to Boston.

▶ At the age of two, John Kennedy fell seriously ill with scarlet fever and nearly died. He was in the hospital, away from his family, for more than three months.

▶ John Kennedy loved to read. As a young boy, he enjoyed adventure stories and tales of fantasy. He chose books about history as a teenager. He especially loved to read about famous world leaders.

▶ As a boy, John's older brother, Joe Jr., announced that he would become president one day. The family thought he would be the politician in the family, and John would be a writer or teacher.

people that he was the best man to run the country. He must work hard to deliver the promises he made during the **campaign.**

Kennedy's entire life had been full of tests and challenges. Even though he grew up with many advantages, life had never been easy. He overcame obstacles throughout his childhood and young adulthood. And when he made up his mind to do something, he did not turn back.

John Fitzgerald Kennedy was born in Brookline, Massachusetts on May 29, 1917. He was the second child of Joseph and Rose Kennedy. Joseph was a wealthy businessman, and Rose was the daughter of one of Boston's best-known politicians. Both Joseph's and Rose's grandparents were **immigrants** from Ireland.

Joseph and Rose practiced the Roman Catholic religion. As Irish Catholics, they and their families faced the harsh **prejudice** of Protestant Bostonians. Rose's father, John Fitzgerald, and Joseph's father, Patrick Kennedy, did not allow the prejudice to discourage them. They worked hard. They also helped other Boston Irish families to get ahead. They achieved this goal by becoming involved in **politics.** John Fitzgerald was mayor of Boston and a U.S. congressman. Patrick Kennedy was a Massachusetts state senator. Through politics, these men passed laws and found ways to improve life for all immigrants.

As a child, John F. Kennedy—known to his family and friends as "Jack"—struggled to keep up with his brother, Joe Jr. This was not an easy task. Joe was two years older. He was healthier, stronger, and more studious. Jack also suffered from many illnesses. Yet these differences did not slow him down. The intelligent, well-coordinated boy never stopped trying to beat his brother at games and sports.

When Jack was 10 years old, his family moved to the suburbs of New York City. His father believed there would be less prejudice there than in Boston. At age 14, Jack attended the Choate School in Connecticut. According to his teachers, he was not a good

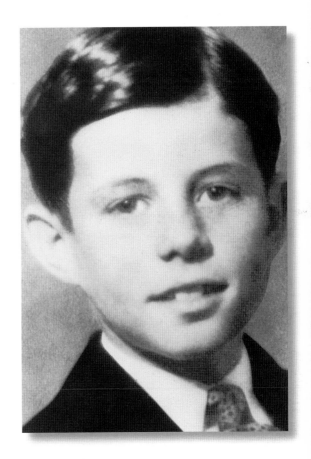

At age 11, Jack loved sports and reading more than schoolwork. He was fun-loving, full of mischief, and made friends easily.

The Kennedy children and their parents were a close-knit family. Even though Joseph Sr. was busy, he was involved in his children's lives. Both parents demanded that their children be the best—in school, in sports, and in all they attempted. This photograph was taken while the family lived in England. From left to right are Eunice, Jack, Rosemary, Jean, Joseph Sr., Edward, Rose, Joe Jr., Pat, Robert, and Kathleen Kennedy.

student. His schoolwork was carelessly done and did not show his true ability. He excelled in sports, however, especially swimming.

After graduating from Choate in 1935, Jack briefly attended Princeton University in New Jersey. A severe illness forced him to drop out, but in 1936, Jack followed Joe Jr. to Harvard College in Massachusetts.

In 1937, President Franklin Roosevelt appointed Joseph Sr. to be the U.S. ambassador to Great Britain. Living in England was an adventure for the Kennedy family. In the

spring of 1939, Europe became Jack's class-room. He toured many countries in central and eastern Europe. He gathered facts for his thesis, a long paper he planned to write during his senior year at Harvard. Jack observed Europe at a crucial time—in the months before the start of World War II. Because his thesis was so well done, he graduated from Harvard College *cum laude* (with honors) in June of 1940.

In 1941, Joe Jr. enlisted in the U.S. Navy. Jack tried to sign up, too, but his poor health caused both the army and the navy to reject him. For five months, Jack worked to make himself stronger. In September of 1941, three months before the United States entered World War II, the navy accepted him.

To Jack's disappointment, he was not assigned to sea duty. He was ordered instead to write news reports in Washington, D.C. In July of 1942, he enrolled in midshipman's school. There he learned all about the navy's PT boats. When the training ended, Jack was not sent overseas as he hoped. He was ordered to teach men how to manage PT boats. He was extremely frustrated.

Interesting Facts

▸ Before Jack's graduation from Choate, his classmates voted him "most likely to succeed." This was meant as a huge joke because Jack was neither a good student nor a school leader. He was often in trouble with the headmaster and his teachers for playing pranks.

▸ Jack said he worked harder on his Harvard thesis than anything else in his life up to that time. It discussed the reasons why World War II began in Europe. At age 23, he became an author. With help from a friend of his father's, his thesis was published as a book called *Why England Slept*.

As would happen many times in Jack's life, his father asked his political friends to help his son. They managed to get Jack a combat assignment. In March of 1943, Jack arrived in the Solomon Islands, where he was commander of *PT 109*. There, in the South Pacific Ocean and its islands, the United States was at war with Japan.

As a child and young adult, Jack was closest to Joe Jr. (left) and his sister Kathleen (center). Joe Jr. was a navy pilot during World War II. In 1944, he was killed when his plane crashed on a secret mission. Jack and Kathleen became even closer as they mourned Joe's death. When Kathleen was killed in a plane crash in 1948, Jack was devastated. He had lost his dearest friend.

LIFE ON A PT BOAT IN THE SOUTH PACIFIC was not very exciting. At least that's what Jack wrote to his sister Kathleen. Night after night, *PT 109* cruised the choppy seas as its crew searched for enemy ships. During the day, the men worked to keep the boat shipshape.

Then, on the night of August 1, 1943, *PT 109* was out on patrol. Its mission was to torpedo Japanese destroyers traveling nearby. The night was completely dark. Suddenly Jack's crew spotted a destroyer racing toward them. Jack turned the wheel sharply so that the men could fire the torpedoes. But it was too late. The Japanese destroyer *Amagiri* struck *PT 109*.

The *Amagiri* was unharmed, but the crash split *PT 109* in two. Two men were killed. Jack severely injured his back. At first, the survivors clung to the wreckage. When rescuers did not arrive, Jack ordered his crew to swim to the nearest island, four miles away.

Jack took charge of Pat McMahon, who was too injured to swim. Jack clenched the rope attached to McMahon's life jacket in his teeth. He then swam to the island towing him. Once the men reached the island, Jack left them to search for U.S. ships. For days he swam from one island to the next, trying to find help. Finally, the native people of the South Sea Islands transported Jack and his crew to safety.

Chapter Two

High Hopes: The Young Politician

Jack Kennedy served three two-year terms in Congress. After his win in 1946, he also won the elections of 1948 and 1950.

JACK RETURNED HOME FROM THE WAR A HERO. But he did not feel heroic. He said he did what any other commander would have done for his crew. One day a newspaper reporter asked him, "How did you become a hero?" Jack joked, "It was easy. They cut my PT boat in half."

1944 was a terrible year for Jack Kennedy. He was in constant pain from his back injury. He was ill from a disease he contracted in the South Pacific. He had a painful operation on his back that failed. Worst of all, Joe Jr. died in a plane crash. Jack grieved with his family. In the following months, Jack dealt with his sadness by working to regain his strength.

A year after Joe Jr.'s death, Joseph Sr. decided that Jack should enter politics.

As Jack said, he had no choice. "It was like being drafted," he recalled. "My father wanted his oldest son in politics." With Joe Jr. gone, Jack was now the oldest son. According to his father, it was Jack's responsibility to carry on for his brother.

After much thought, Jack agreed to aim for a political career in Massachusetts. His family was firmly committed to the Democratic Party, one of the nation's two most powerful **political parties.** Jack and his

Kennedy was not a skilled public speaker at the beginning of his political career. He found it difficult to talk to a crowd without a written speech. With careful study and practice, speech coaches, and talented speechwriters, Kennedy became one of the greatest public speakers of the 20th century.

15

▸ In 1952, Kohei
Hanami, the former
commander of the
Amagiri, read an article
about Kennedy in *Time*
magazine. In that
article, Kennedy said
that he had searched for
Hanami while on a trip
to Japan. Hanami was
impressed that Kennedy
wished goodwill to
his former enemy. In
a letter, Hanami told
Kennedy that he
believed the senator
would encourage
friendship between
Japan and the United
States, as well as peace
around the world.

▸ Kennedy was
awarded the Navy
and Marine Corps
Medal for his heroism
during World War II.

father decided that he should run for a seat
in the House of Representatives, part of the
U.S. Congress. They knew it would be an
uphill battle. Jack was unknown and had no
political experience. Boston politicians said
that the poor working people of his **district**
would never vote for a "rich kid."

But Jack Kennedy proved them wrong.
He never stopped campaigning. As long as
there were voters to talk to, he kept going. In
the primary election, he ran against nine other
Democrats. In a primary election, voters cast
ballots to decide who will be the **candidate** of
a particular political party. Jack won, receiving
42% of the votes. This was a huge percentage
in a 10-person race. In November, he easily
defeated the Republican candidate. At age 29,
Kennedy became one of the youngest people
to be elected to Congress.

Kennedy served in the House from 1947
to 1951. He concentrated on helping the
people in his district. The lack of low-cost
housing in Boston concerned him. He worked
hard to make laws that would allow thousands
of families to live in a house or an apartment
of their own. He pushed for higher wages for

16

As a congressman, Kennedy traveled in Europe and in eastern Asia. On these trips, he learned much about the governments and business affairs of foreign nations. He knew he would need this knowledge if he became a U.S. senator.

workers. He also wanted the government to provide more aid to the elderly. He supported a **bill** that would permit immigrants from central and eastern Europe to come to the United States.

But Kennedy's work in Congress was not all he had hoped. He had little time to pursue what most interested him—foreign affairs, which are matters involving other countries. For this goal, he would need a

▶ While Senator Kennedy was recovering from back surgery, he began writing a book about eight U.S. political leaders who showed great courage. The best-selling book, *Profiles in Courage,* was published in 1956 and won the Pulitzer Prize in 1957.

▶ Early in 1960, Kennedy decided that he must improve his public speaking. He worked with a drama coach. This specialist gave him lots of voice exercises. One routine was to bark like a seal for two minutes every-day. Kennedy liked to do this while in the bathtub.

seat in the U.S. Senate, which is the other half of Congress.

In November of 1952, Kennedy won a hard-fought campaign for the Senate. His entire family helped. His younger brother, Robert Kennedy, was his campaign manager. "Bobby" was an excellent organizer. Like Jack, he had a powerful fighting spirit that never quit.

At the 1956 Democratic Party Convention, Kennedy became known to millions of Americans for the first time. The Democratic Convention is an important meeting where members of the party choose their presidential candidate. Adlai Stevenson was the party's choice that year. Kennedy almost became his vice presidential running mate, but in the end was not chosen.

Kennedy became a member of the Senate Committee on Foreign Relations in 1957. He had long dreamed of winning this position. While on the committee, he strongly supported U.S. aid to poor nations in Asia and Africa.

In 1958 and 1959, Kennedy worked tire-lessly to help American workers. He pushed through a bill that increased unemployment insurance, which would help workers who lost their jobs. He also tried to make laws to stop the managers of **labor unions** from wasting the money of American workers. And in addition to all of his work in the Senate, he prepared to run for president in the next election.

In 1960, Kennedy won seven primary elections and lost three. At the Democratic Convention, he won the **nomination** on the first ballot. In his acceptance speech, he told Americans how his "New Frontier" program would improve their lives.

He chose Senator Lyndon Baines Johnson of Texas as his vice presidential running mate. Johnson was the powerful leader of the Senate Democrats. Kennedy selected him because he would capture the votes of southern Democrats, votes he would need to win the election.

Kennedy's early years as a senator were difficult. He had the spirit and ambition to be a great leader. His body was the only thing holding him back, and it frustrated him deeply.

▸ After the first
Kennedy-Nixon
debate, most people
who listened to it on
the radio thought
that Nixon won.
Most who watched
the debate on tele-
vision thought that
Kennedy won.

Kennedy and the Republican candidate, Vice President Richard Nixon, participated in four **debates.** These were broadcast on television and radio. Both men showed that they were knowledgeable and intelligent. But Kennedy had one advantage: He was a natural on television. He appeared relaxed, confident, and in command.

In 1953, Senator Kennedy married Jacqueline Lee "Jackie" Bouvier. Like Jack, she was well educated, intelligent, and from a wealthy family. Jackie loved literature, music, and art. Jack Kennedy fascinated her from the moment she met him.

DURING MOST OF HIS years in Congress, Jack was weak, underweight, and exhausted. In 1947, doctors discovered that he had a serious illness called Addison's disease. There was no treatment or cure. The doctors believed that Jack did not have long to live. But Jack decided to keep working and hid the fact that he had the disease. He did not want people to think that he wasn't strong enough to handle his duties. This was important, because he planned to begin a campaign for higher office. This photograph shows Congressman Kennedy touring the Boston waterfront despite severe illness.

In 1950, doctors developed a medicine for Addison's disease. Jack felt stronger than he had in years, but the drug was not a cure. He struggled with the illness for the rest of his life.

As Jack felt stronger, his back pain became worse. He was often unable to walk without crutches. He needed surgery, but doctors warned him that it would threaten his life. Surgery was risky because of his Addison's disease. Jack wanted the operation. Only if his back pain were eased would life be worth living.

After the surgery in October of 1954, an infection roared through his body and he nearly died. With Jackie by his side, Jack began a long recovery. His back failed to heal, however. He risked another, more successful operation. In May of 1955, he returned to the Senate. He was finally strong enough to do the job.

Chapter THREE

The Crisis Years

Kennedy's wit, his ability to make fun of himself, and his hard work made him very popular.

ON JANUARY 20, 1961, JOHN F. KENNEDY was **inaugurated** president of the United States. He was determined to launch his New Frontier program right away. His first order sent food to poverty-stricken areas. With the help of Congress, he signed bills into law that helped poor working people. One law raised the minimum wage to $1.25 per hour. Another set aside government dollars to improve poor communities. Kennedy also succeeded in pushing through a multi-billion-dollar housing bill. This helped thousands of Americans to rent or own their homes.

As Kennedy was working to fulfill his campaign promises, the country faced one crisis after another. Suddenly the new presi-

dent found himself involved in the worst crises of the Cold War.

The Cold War was not a war in the usual sense. No soldiers or sailors fought in battle. The Cold War was a conflict between the United States and the **Soviet Union.** The Soviet Union was trying to spread its system of government, called **communism,** to other nations. The United States was determined to stop communists from taking over other countries. It helped **democracies** protect

At his inauguration, Kennedy began his 1,037 days as president by giving an unforgettable speech. He urged Americans to join together to work for freedom and lasting peace at home and around the world.

23

▸ Kennedy received much approval for founding the Peace Corps. This organization sends U.S. volunteers to help people in poor communities in Asia, Latin America, and Africa. Kennedy hoped that the Peace Corps would spread peace and goodwill throughout the world.

▸ Kennedy was a constant reader. He read at least four newspapers every morning with his breakfast. He read magazines as well. He also found the time to read three or four books every week. Kennedy was a speed reader. He once estimated that he could read 1,000 words per minute.

their governments from communism. It also encouraged other countries to become democratic like the United States.

Kennedy's first Cold War crisis was his biggest failure as president. In April of 1961, the United States began an invasion of Cuba, a small island nation near Florida. Cuba was ruled by the Communist **dictator** Fidel Castro. The Bay of Pigs invasion was supposed to remove Castro from power and end Communist rule in Cuba. But the mission was a disaster.

Kennedy blamed himself for the failure. Military leaders and other advisors had told him that the invasion would likely succeed. Kennedy believed that he should have realized it would never work. He vowed to make decisions more carefully in the future.

Despite the disaster, Kennedy was convinced that Cuba must be freed from communism. It was too close to the United States mainland and too friendly with the Soviet Union for U.S. safety. Through a plan called Operation Mongoose, U.S. government agents interfered with Cuba's business with other nations. The U.S. Navy patrolled

Fidel Castro became the leader of Cuba in 1959. In 1961, under his dictatorship, Cuba's government became communist.

the waters around Cuba. The U.S. government also arranged to have Castro **assassinated,** although this plan did not succeed.

Castro grew alarmed. He believed that the United States was about to invade his country. He asked the Soviet leader Nikita Khrushchev for help. The Soviet Union sent **nuclear missiles** to Cuba—weapons that could strike the United States. The building of missile sites triggered the Cuban Missile Crisis in October of 1962.

Kennedy knew that the United States could not allow nuclear missiles in Cuba

▶ In May of 1961, Kennedy announced, "I believe that this nation should commit itself to … landing a man on the moon before this decade is out." To prepare for this goal, NASA's Mercury Program launched six astronauts into space from 1961 to 1963. Alan Shepard was the first American astronaut to blast off. His flight lasted only 15 minutes.

25

▶ Kennedy chose his
brother Robert, a
lawyer, to be attorney
general. He did not
want to select Bobby
at first, but their father
convinced Jack that
he needed his brother.
His father said that he
must have at least one
advisor who he could
trust completely. As
attorney general,
Robert led the U.S.
Justice Department
and served as a member
of the president's cab-
inet, the group of
people who advise
the president.

because it was too dangerous. But getting rid
of them presented a huge problem. If the
United States entered Cuba or bombed the
missile sites, the Soviet Union might declare
war. Warfare in the 1960s was extremely
risky. An ordinary battle could turn into a
nuclear war. Such a war could destroy not
only the United States and the Soviet Union,
but other parts of the world as well.

For days, Kennedy and his advisors
considered what to do. Finally, the president
made his decision. He ordered a naval blockade of Cuba. This meant that the U.S. Navy
would stop Soviet ships from delivering
materials to the missile sites. Kennedy
believed that this was the safest way to put an
end to the crisis. He then demanded that the
Soviet ships turn around and go home.

It was a terrifying time for the American
people. What if Soviet leader Nikita Khrushchev
ordered the ships to fight their way through
the blockade? Would a nuclear war result?
The entire world watched and waited.

Khrushchev ordered the Soviet ships to
turn away from Cuba. He offered to make a
deal with Kennedy. The Soviet missiles would

leave Cuba if the United States promised never to invade Cuba and to remove its missiles from Turkey. Kennedy agreed. The Cuban Missile Crisis was over.

In the midst of these Cold War emergencies, another enormous struggle was heating up, this time in the United States. The **Civil Rights Movement** was gaining power. In much of the South, African Americans were protesting **segregation** and their lack of civil rights, which are the rights guaranteed to American citizens by the U.S. Constitution. Civil rights include the freedom to vote, freedom of speech, freedom of religion, and the right to be treated equally according to the laws of the nation.

In 1961 and 1962, Kennedy respected the goals of civil rights leaders. But he did not want the rights of African Americans to be a big issue. His relationship with Congress held him back. After his first few months as president, Congress would not pass most of

"Vigor" was a word that Kennedy used often. To be a successful leader, he believed that a president must be full of vigor— strong, tough, energetic, and full of brilliant ideas and plans.

▶ Redecorating the White House was a special project of Jackie Kennedy's. To furnish the mansion, she collected historic American furniture and artwork from all over the country. The first lady said that the White House belonged to the American people. She believed that they should have the opportunity to take pride in it and enjoy its beauty.

his bills. The Republicans and southern Democrats in Congress joined forces to block the bills he hoped would pass.

Kennedy feared that if he strongly supported civil rights, he would never convince southern Democrats to pass his laws. Not only that, he was sure white southern voters would not vote for his reelection in 1964.

The disturbing events of 1962 and 1963 would force Kennedy to change his mind about the Civil Rights Movement.

Jack and Jackie's children made the White House a lively place. Caroline was born in 1957, and John Jr. was born a few weeks after the 1960 election. August 9, 1963, was a tragic day for the Kennedy family. A third child, Patrick, died of a serious lung disease. He was just two days old.

28

ONE MAJOR "BATTLEGROUND" of the Cold War was the city of Berlin in East Germany. After the defeat of the Nazis in World War II, Germany was divided into two coun-tries. One was the democratic nation of West Germany. The other was communist East Germany. The old German capital of Berlin was also divided in two. It became the West German city of West Berlin and the East German capital of East Berlin. The people of West Berlin were left with a big problem: How could they stay a part of democratic West Germany while surrounded by communist East Germany?

East Germany also had a problem. Its citizens were escaping to West Berlin to find freedom and a better life. In 1961, the stream of runaways became a flood. To stop them, communist leaders ordered that a concrete wall be built between the two cities. East German troops patrolled the Berlin Wall to make sure that no one escaped to West Berlin.

East German soldiers then blocked the one free road leading into and out of West Berlin. Kennedy was determined that West Berlin remain a free city. He ordered U.S. troops to march on the road. The East Germans did not try to stop the U.S. Army, and the road remained open. The Berlin Wall remained, but West Berlin did not become part of communist East Germany.

On June 26, 1963, Kennedy visited West Berlin. More than half its citizens came out to welcome him. At the Berlin Wall, Kennedy told them, "Freedom has many difficulties and democracy is not perfect, but we have never had to put a wall up to keep our people in." The cheers of the crowd were deafening.

29

Chapter FOUR

Triumph and Tragedy

President Kennedy worried that if one nation became communist, others would follow. Vietnam was a trouble spot for him. Its government was moving toward communism. By November of 1963, Kennedy had ordered more than 16,000 U.S. troops to Vietnam.

IN 1961 AND 1962, PRESIDENT KENNEDY wished that the Civil Rights Movement would proceed more slowly. He had so many world crises that demanded his attention. He was also struggling to push new laws through Congress, laws that would improve the lives of all Americans.

But the Civil Rights Movement could not wait. African Americans in the South had waited hundreds of years for their freedom—for the same civil rights that every white American took for granted. Civil rights leaders told Kennedy that waiting was not only impossible, it was unthinkable.

In 1962, James Meredith, a young African American, obtained a U.S. court order. It told the all-white University of

President Kennedy depended on his wife for her political know-how and her gracious manner with foreign leaders. In 1962, the president sent Jackie on a mission to India and Pakistan. In India, she met with politician Indira Gandhi, who later served as India's prime minister from 1966 to 1977 and from 1980 to 1984.

Mississippi to accept him as a student. The university refused. Kennedy demanded that the school admit Meredith. He sent U.S. marshals to protect Meredith and to make sure that no one blocked his way.

At least 2,000 white rioters protested Meredith's presence. More than 160 marshals and several hundred people in the crowd were

Interesting Facts

▶ In 1962, Kennedy's youngest brother Edward "Ted" Kennedy was elected to the U.S. Senate from Massachusetts. At age 30, Ted became the youngest person ever elected to the Senate.

President Kennedy shakes hands with Astronaut John Glenn, who received the NASA Distinguished Service Award for his space journey. Glenn was the first American to orbit the Earth on February 20, 1962. Years later, Glenn became a U.S. senator. In 1998, at age 77, he was a crew member on the space shuttle Discovery.

wounded. Two people were killed. Kennedy sen thousands of troops to keep the peace.

In May of 1963, civil rights protesters—including many schoolchildren—marched in Birmingham, Alabama. They wanted equal rights and an end to segregation. Even though they protested peacefully, the Birmingham police fought back. They used dogs and water gushing from fire hoses to attack the marchers.

In June of 1963, African American students were blocked from enrolling at the University of Alabama. Once more, rioters threatened the peace. On June 11, Kennedy ordered U.S. marshals to protect the students as they registered for summer classes.

These events opened Kennedy's eyes. He was shocked by the racial violence and hatred. He was horrified by the cruelty of police. He realized that civil rights for African Americans could not be postponed any longer.

On the afternoon of June 11, 1963, President Kennedy told his aides, "I want to go on television tonight." At eight o'clock, he delivered his most stirring speech on civil rights. He told the American people that "this nation … will not be fully free until all its citizens are free." He said he planned to send a civil rights bill to Congress. This law would allow African Americans to be served in all public places—restaurants, hotels, theaters, and stores. It would end segregation in public schools. And it would make sure that all African Americans were permitted to vote.

Kennedy knew that he was risking his political future. By supporting civil rights, he was certain to lose the approval of white southerners. He knew that he would have a tough time being reelected in 1964 without their votes. But he did not turn away from what he knew was right. He would see to it that the Civil Rights Act became law.

Interesting Facts

▸ For his back pain, Kennedy received shots of a painkiller called novocaine five or six times a day. They were injected into his back. Kennedy did not care that the shots were extremely painful. He always felt much better for two hours after each treatment.

▸ Of all the character traits he got from his family, President Kennedy said that curiosity was the one he most cherished.

On August 28, 1963, 200,000 civil rights marchers traveled to Washington, D.C. They demanded jobs and freedom. They called on Congress to pass Kennedy's Civil Rights Bill. Martin Luther King Jr. delivered his famous "I Have a Dream" speech. After the March on Washington, Kennedy met with King and other civil rights leaders. Kennedy believed the success of the march would help pass his Civil Rights Bill.

Kennedy said that the most important achievement of his presidency was the Nuclear Test-Ban Treaty. Years of hard work and **compromise** with the Soviet Union went into this effort. In the summer of 1963, the United States, the Soviet Union, and the United Kingdom promised to end above-ground and underwater testing of nuclear weapons. They agreed that they would no longer poison the air or the oceans with these tests. Starting on October 10, 1963, they would test nuclear weapons underground.

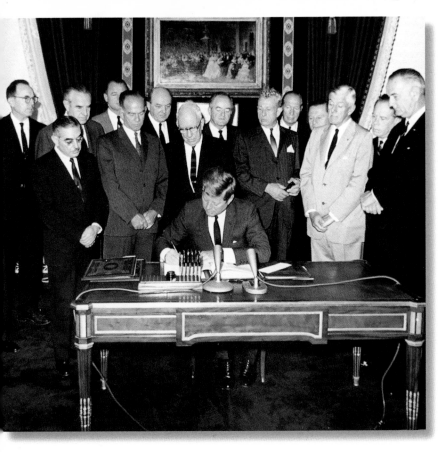

The prospect of a nuclear war hung over Kennedy's years as president. In 1961, he said, "The weapons of war must be abolished before they abolish us." Here, during his final months as president, he is shown signing the treaty that was a first step toward this goal.

In late November of 1963, President and Mrs. Kennedy traveled to Texas. Kennedy hoped that the visit would encourage Texans to vote for him in the 1964 election. While riding through the streets of Dallas on November 22, two shots rang out and killed the president.

The entire nation was plunged into mourning. President Kennedy had been so full of life. He was always bursting with ideas for the future of the country. It was very hard for Americans to accept that he was gone.

Interesting Facts

▶ Kennedy made audio tape recordings of cabinet meetings, discussions with his staff, his telephone calls, and nearly every word spoken in the Oval Office. These tapes reveal the problems the president faced and the decisions he made. The tapes are stored at the JFK Library in Boston, Massachusetts, where historians and students may study them.

▶ Robert Kennedy
resigned as U.S.
attorney general in
September of 1964.
He was elected to the
U.S. Senate from
New York State in
November of 1964.
In March of 1968, he
launched his campaign
for the presidency,
following in his
brother's footsteps.
Then on June 5,
tragedy struck the
family again. After
winning the California
primary election,
Robert was assassinated
by a man named
Sirhan Bishara Sirhan.

Shortly after Kennedy was pronounced dead, Vice President Lyndon Johnson was sworn in as president. In the months ahead, President Johnson convinced Congress to pass much of Kennedy's New Frontier legislation. The most important was the Civil Rights Act of 1964. At long last, the United States was one step closer to Kennedy's dream of freedom for all Americans.

Millions of Americans and people all over the world watched President Kennedy's funeral on television. John Jr., who turned three years old that day, saluted his father's coffin as it rolled by.

NEARLY 40 YEARS AFTER PRESIDENT KENNEDY'S assassination, people still question the cause of his death. Many Americans believe that Kennedy was killed by one man, Lee Harvey Oswald. Others are convinced that his death was the result of a **conspiracy.**

What do the experts think? In 1964, the Warren Commission—the official government investigation—examined the evidence. They decided that Oswald fired the shots that killed the president.

In the 1970s, a startling discovery was made. In 1964, the Federal Bureau of Investigation (FBI) and the Central Intelligence Agency (CIA) did not tell the Warren investigators all they knew about Oswald's life.

Why did they withhold evidence? At the time, FBI and CIA officials did not give information to other government groups unless it was necessary. They knew that their facts would not change the Warren Commission's conclusion that Oswald was the only killer. As a result, they did not reveal all they knew.

Americans were disturbed by the actions of the FBI and the CIA. Some people believed that they were hiding facts about Kennedy's death. In the late 1970s, a Congressional committee studied the assassination. They agreed with the Warren Commission that Oswald was the only killer. The American people were not convinced. In 1983, 74% of Americans believed in an assassination conspiracy.

What do the experts believe today? Most experts who have studied the case say that Oswald was the only assassin. Nevertheless, other experts and many Americans believe that this is not the case.

1917 On May 29, John Fitzgerald "Jack" Kennedy is born in Brookline, Massachusetts.

1935 Kennedy graduates from the Choate School. In the fall, he attends Princeton University.

1936 Kennedy enrolls at Harvard College.

1937 Joseph Kennedy Sr. is appointed U.S. ambassador to Great Britain. Jack spends school vacations in London with his family.

1940 Kennedy graduates from Harvard College in June.

1941 Kennedy enlists in the U.S. Navy. The Japanese attack Pearl Harbor in Hawaii on December 7. The United States declares war on Japan on December 8.

1943 Kennedy arrives in the Solomon Islands in the South Pacific on March 28. A Japanese destroyer sinks *PT 109* on the night of August 1. At the end of December, he returns to the United States.

1946 Kennedy is elected to Congress in November.

1947 On January 3, Kennedy begins his two-year term as a member of the U.S. House of Representatives. In October, doctors in England discover that he has Addison's disease.

1948 Kennedy is reelected to Congress in November.

1950 Kennedy begins a new treatment for Addison's disease. In November, he is elected to serve a third term in Congress.

1952 Kennedy is elected to the U.S. Senate.

1953 Kennedy is sworn in as senator on January 3. On September 12, he marries Jacqueline Lee Bouvier in Newport, Rhode Island.

1954 On October 21, Kennedy has an operation on his back. Days later, he falls into a coma and nearly dies. A long recovery begins.

1955 On February 11, Kennedy has another back operation. In May, he returns to the Senate and is able to walk without crutches.

1956 Kennedy's *Profiles in Courage* is published in January. At the Democratic National Convention in August, he makes a bid for the vice presidential nomination. He comes close but does not win the nomination. He becomes known to millions of Americans when he gives the speech that nominates Adlai Stevenson.

1958 Kennedy is reelected to the U.S. Senate by the largest number of votes in Massachusetts history. He prepares to run for president in 1960.

1960 Kennedy defeats Richard Nixon in the presidential election on November 8.

1961 Kennedy is inaugurated the 35th president on January 20. He forms the Peace Corps on March 1. The Bay of Pigs invasion begins on April 17 and fails within days. On May 5, the United States sends Astronaut Alan Shepard on the nation's first manned space flight. Kennedy and Nikita Khrushchev meet in Vienna, Austria, on June 3 and 4. In August, Khrushchev orders the building of the Berlin Wall. Kennedy orders troops to safeguard the free road in and out of West Berlin. Late in the year, Kennedy orders troops to Vietnam.

1962 In February, Kennedy sends more troops to Vietnam. A total of 12,000 military personnel serve in that country. Astronaut John Glenn becomes the first American to orbit the Earth on February 20. On September 30, 2,000 rioters protest the presence of African American student James Meredith at the University of Mississippi. The next day, he is successfully enrolled at the school. The Cuban Missile Crisis begins on October 14 when U.S. spy planes observe missiles in Cuba. On October 28, the crisis is resolved.

1963 Kennedy travels to West Berlin and delivers a speech at the Berlin Wall on June 26. On August 28, more than 200,000 people take part in the March on Washington. The Nuclear Test-Ban Treaty goes into effect on October 10. President and Mrs. Kennedy leave for Texas on November 21. Kennedy is shot and killed in Dallas on November 22. Vice President Lyndon Johnson is sworn in as the nation's 36th president on November 22. On November 24, Lee Harvey Oswald, Kennedy's assassin, is shot and killed by Jack Ruby.

1964 President Johnson signs the Civil Rights Bill on July 2.

assassinate (uh-SASS-ih-nayt)
Assassinate means to murder someone, especially a well-known person. President John F. Kennedy was assassinated on November 22, 1963.

bill (BILL)
A bill is an idea for a new law that is presented to a group of lawmakers. Kennedy supported a bill that would permit immigrants from Europe to come to the United States.

campaign (kam-PAYN)
A campaign is the process of running for an election, including activities such as giving speeches or attending rallies. Kennedy tried to keep promises he made during his campaign.

candidate (KAN-dih-det)
A candidate is a person running in an election. In a primary election, voters decide who will be the candidate of a political party.

Civil Rights Movement (SIV-el RYTZ MOOV-ment)
The Civil Rights Movement was the name given to the struggle for equal rights for African Americans in the United States during the 1950s and 1960s. The events of 1962 and 1963 forced Kennedy to become involved in the Civil Rights Movement.

communism (KOM-yeh-niz-em)
Communism is a system of government in which the central government, not the people, holds all the power, and there is no private ownership of property. During the Cold War, Americans feared that communism would spread throughout the world.

compromise (KOM-pruh-myz)
A compromise is a way to settle a disagreement in which both sides give up part of what they want. The Nuclear Test-Ban Treaty was a compromise between the Soviet Union and the United States.

conspiracy (kon-SPEER-uh-see)
A conspiracy is an action by two or more people to carry out a crime. Many Americans believe the plot to kill President Kennedy was a conspiracy.

debates (dee-BAYTZ)
Debates are formal meetings in which two people discuss a topic. Kennedy and Richard Nixon participated in four debates before the presidential election of 1960.

democracies (deh-MOK-ruh-seez)
Democracies are nations in which the people control the government by electing their own leaders. The United States helped democracies protect their governments from communism.

Glossary Terms

dictator (DIK-tay-tor)
A dictator is a ruler with complete power over a country. Fidel Castro has been the dictator of Cuba since 1959.

district (DIS-trikt)
A district is a small area. Some politicians did not think voters in Kennedy's district would vote him into the House of Representatives.

immigrants (IM-ih-grentz)
Immigrants are people who leave one country to live in another. Millions of Irish immigrants came to the United States during the 1800s.

inaugurate (ih-NAWG-yuh-rayt)
When politicians are inaugurated, they formally enter an elected office. John F. Kennedy was inaugurated on January 20, 1961.

labor unions (LAY-bor YOON-yenz)
Labor unions are groups of workers who join together to demand better treatment. Senator Kennedy tried to pass a law to stop labor unions from wasting their members' money.

nomination (nom-ih-NAY-shun)
If someone receives a nomination, he or she is chosen by a political party to run for an office, such as the presidency. Kennedy won the Democratic Party's presidential nomination in 1960.

nuclear missiles (NOO-klee-ur MISS-ulz)
Nuclear missiles are nuclear weapons that are launched into space and then fall to Earth to hit their target. The Soviet Union sent nuclear missiles to Cuba in 1962.

political parties (puh-LIT-ih-kul PAR-teez)
Political parties are groups of people who share similar ideas about how to run a government. The Democratic Party is a powerful political party.

politics (PAWL-ih-tiks)
Politics refers to the actions and practices of the government. Kennedy's grandfather's were involved in politics.

prejudice (PREJ-uh-des)
Prejudice is a negative feeling or opinion about someone without a good reason. Irish Catholics once faced prejudice from Protestants.

segregation (seh-grih-GAY-shun)
Segregation was the policy and practice of separating Americans—white and black—into two groups, according to race. Civil rights leaders wanted to outlaw segregation.

Soviet Union (SOH-vee-et YOON-yen)
The Soviet Union was a communist country that stretched from eastern Europe across Asia to the Pacific Ocean. It separated into several smaller countries in 1991.

Our PRESIDENTS

President	Birthplace	Life Dates	Term	Political Party	First Lady
George Washington	Virginia	1732–1799	1789–1797	None	Martha Dandridge Custis Washington
John Adams	Massachusetts	1735–1826	1797–1801	Federalist	Abigail Smith Adams
Thomas Jefferson	Virginia	1743–1826	1801–1809	Democratic-Republican	widower
James Madison	Virginia	1751–1836	1809–1817	Democratic-Republican	Dolley Payne Todd Madison
James Monroe	Virginia	1758–1831	1817–1825	Democratic-Republican	Elizabeth "Eliza" Kortright Monroe
John Quincy Adams	Massachusetts	1767–1848	1825–1829	Democratic-Republican	Louisa Catherine Johnson Adams
Andrew Jackson	South Carolina	1767–1845	1829–1837	Democrat	widower
Martin Van Buren	New York	1782–1862	1837–1841	Democrat	widower
William Henry Harrison	Virginia	1773–1841	1841	Whig	Anna Tuthill Symmes Harrison
John Tyler	Virginia	1790–1862	1841–1845	Whig	Letitia Christian Tyler / Julia Gardiner Tyler
James Polk	North Carolina	1795–1849	1845–1849	Democrat	Sarah Childress Polk

Our PRESIDENTS

President	Birthplace	Life Dates	Term	Political Party	First Lady
Zachary Taylor	Virginia	1784–1850	1849–1850	Whig	Margaret Mackall Smith Taylor
Millard Fillmore	New York	1800–1874	1850–1853	Whig	Abigail Powers Fillmore
Franklin Pierce	New Hampshire	1804–1869	1853–1857	Democrat	Jane Means Appleton Pierce
James Buchanan	Pennsylvania	1791–1868	1857–1861	Democrat	never married
Abraham Lincoln	Kentucky	1809–1865	1861–1865	Republican	Mary Todd Lincoln
Andrew Johnson	North Carolina	1808–1875	1865–1869	Democrat	Eliza McCardle Johnson
Ulysses S. Grant	Ohio	1822–1885	1869–1877	Republican	Julia Dent Grant
Rutherford B. Hayes	Ohio	1822–1893	1877–1881	Republican	Lucy Ware Webb Hayes
James A. Garfield	Ohio	1831–1881	1881	Republican	Lucretia Rudolph Garfield
Chester A. Arthur	Vermont	1829–1886	1881–1885	Republican	widower
Grover Cleveland	New Jersey	1837–1908	1885–1889	Democrat	Frances Folsom Cleveland

Our PRESIDENTS

President	Birthplace	Life Dates	Term	Political Party	First Lady
Benjamin Harrison	Ohio	1833–1901	1889–1893	Republican	Caroline Lavina Scott Harrison
Grover Cleveland	New Jersey	1837–1908	1893–1897	Democrat	Frances Folsom Cleveland
William McKinley	Ohio	1843–1901	1897–1901	Republican	Ida Saxton McKinley
Theodore Roosevelt	New York	1858–1919	1901–1909	Republican	Edith Kermit Carow Roosevelt
William Howard Taft	Ohio	1857–1930	1909–1913	Republican	Helen Herron Taft
Woodrow Wilson	Virginia	1856–1924	1913–1921	Democrat	Ellen L. Axson Wilson Edith Bolling Galt Wilson
Warren G. Harding	Ohio	1865–1923	1921–1923	Republican	Florence Kling De Wolfe Harding
Calvin Coolidge	Vermont	1872–1933	1923–1929	Republican	Grace Anna Goodhue Coolidge
Herbert Hoover	Iowa	1874–1964	1929–1933	Republican	Lou Henry Hoover
Franklin D. Roosevelt	New York	1882–1945	1933–1945	Democrat	Anna Eleanor Roosevelt Roosevelt
Harry S. Truman	Missouri	1884–1972	1945–1953	Democrat	Elizabeth "Bess" Virginia Wallace Truman

Our PRESIDENTS

President	Birthplace	Life Dates	Term	Political Party	First Lady
Dwight D. Eisenhower	Texas	1890–1969	1953–1961	Republican	Mamie Geneva Doud Eisenhower
John F. Kennedy	Massachusetts	1917–1963	1961–1963	Democrat	Jacqueline Lee Bouvier Kennedy
Lyndon Baines Johnson	Texas	1908–1973	1963–1969	Democrat	Claudia "Lady Bird" Alta Taylor Johnson
Richard M. Nixon	California	1913–1994	1969–1974	Republican	Thelma "Pat" Catherine Patricia Ryan Nixon
Gerald R. Ford	Nebraska	1913–	1974–1977	Republican	Elizabeth "Betty" Bloomer Warren Ford
James Earl Carter	Georgia	1924–	1977–1981	Democrat	Rosalynn Smith Carter
Ronald Reagan	Illinois	1911–2004	1981–1989	Republican	Nancy Davis Reagan
George Bush	Massachusetts	1924–	1989–1993	Republican	Barbara Pierce Bush
William J. Clinton	Arkansas	1946–	1993–2001	Democrat	Hillary Rodham Clinton
George W. Bush	Connecticut	1946–	2001–	Republican	Laura Welch Bush

Presidential FACTS

Qualifications

To run for president, a candidate must
- be at least 35 years old
- be a citizen who was born in the United States
- have lived in the United States for 14 years

Term of Office

A president's term of office is four years. No president can stay in office for more than two terms.

Election Date

The presidential election takes place every four years on the first Tuesday of November.

Inauguration Date

Presidents are inaugurated on January 20.

Oath of Office

I do solemnly swear I will faithfully execute the office of the President of the United States and will to the best of my ability preserve, protect, and defend the Constitution of the United States.

Write a Letter to the President

One of the best things about being a U.S. citizen is that Americans get to participate in their government. They can speak out if they feel government leaders aren't doing their jobs. They can also praise leaders who are going the extra mile. Do you have something you'd like the president to do? Should the president worry more about the environment and encourage people to recycle? Should the government spend more money on our schools? You can write a letter to the president to say how you feel!

1600 Pennsylvania Avenue
Washington, D.C. 20500

You can even send an e-mail to: president@whitehouse.gov

For Further INFORMATION

Internet Sites

Visit the John F. Kennedy Library and Museum in Boston, Massachusetts:
http://www.cs.umb.edu/jfklibrary/index.htm

Learn more about President Kennedy:
http://www.americanpresidents.org/
http://gi.grolier.com/presidents/nbk/bios/35pkenn.html
http://gi.grolier.com/presidents/ea/bios/35pkenn.html

Learn more about the Nixon-Kennedy debates:
http://www.si.edu/resource/faq/nmah/political.htm

View a photo history of John Fitzgerald Kennedy:
http://www.historyplace.com/kennedy/gallery.htm

Learn more about all the presidents and visit the White House:
http://www.whitehouse.gov/WH/glimpse/presidents/html/presidents.html
http://www.thepresidency.org/presinfo.htm
http://www.americanpresidents.org/

Books

Hakim, Joy. *All the People 1945–1998*. New York: Oxford University Press, 1999.

Hampton, Wilborn. *Kennedy Assassinated! The World Mourns: A Reporter's Story*. Cambridge, MA: Candlewick Press, 1997.

Harrison, Barbara, and Daniel Terris. *A Twilight Struggle: The Life of John Fitzgerald Kennedy*. New York: Lothrop, Lee & Shepard, 1992.

Kent, Zachary. *John F. Kennedy*. Chicago: Childrens Press, 1987.

King, Casey. *Oh, Freedom!: Kids Talk about the Civil Rights Movement with the People Who Made It Happen*. New York: Knopf, 1997.

Randall, Marta. *John F. Kennedy*. New York: Chelsea House, 1988.

Turck, Mary. *The Civil Rights Movement for Kids: A History with 21 Activities*. Chicago: Chicago Review Press, 2000.

STORRS LIBRARY
693 Longmeadow Street
Longmeadow, MA 01106

Index

African Americans, civil rights of, 27-28, 30-34, 39
Amagiri, 13, 16

Bay of Pigs invasion, 24, 39
Berlin, 29, 39
Bouvier, Jacqueline Lee. *See* Kennedy, Jacqueline Lee Bouvier.

Castro, Fidel, 24-25
Civil Rights Act of 1964, 33, 36
Civil Rights Movement, 27-28, 30-34, 39
Cold War, 23-27, 29, 39
communism, 23, 24
Cuba, 24-25, 39
Cuban Missile Crisis, 25-27, 39

Democratic National Convention, 18-19, 39
Democratic Party, 15, 16, 19, 28

East and West Germany, 29, 39

Fitzgerald, John F., 8-9

Gandhi, Indira, 31
Glenn, John, 32, 39

Hanami, Kohei, 16

immigrants, 8-9, 17
Irish Catholics, 8

Japan, 12, 13, 38
JFK Library, 35
Johnson, Lyndon Baines, 19, 36, 39

Kennedy, Edward Moore, 31
Kennedy, Jacqueline Lee Bouvier, 20-21, 28, 31, 38-39
Kennedy, John, Jr., 28, 36
Kennedy, John Fitzgerald
    Addison's disease, 21, 38
    assassination of, 35, 37, 39
    back injuries, 14, 18, 21, 33, 38
    birth of, 8, 38
    childhood of, 9
    education of, 9-11, 38
    election of, 6-7, 39
    illnesses of, 8-9
    inauguration of, 22-23
    marriage of, 20, 38

navy career, 11-13, 38
    nomination for president, 19
    as senator, 18-19, 38-39
    as U.S. representative, 16-17, 38
Kennedy, Joseph, Jr., 8-12, 14-15
Kennedy, Joseph Patrick, 8-10, 14, 38
Kennedy, Kathleen, 12
Kennedy, Patrick J., 8-9
Kennedy, Robert Francis, 18, 26, 36
Kennedy, Rose Fitzgerald, 8
Khrushchev, Nikita, 25-27, 39
King, Martin Luther, Jr., 34

labor unions, 19

McMahon, Pat, 13
Meredith, James, 30-31, 39

New Frontier program, 19, 22, 36
Nixon, Richard, 6-7, 20, 39
Nuclear Test-Ban Treaty, 34-35, 39
nuclear weapons, 25-27, 34-35, 39

Operation Mongoose, 24-25
Oswald, Lee Harvey, 37, 39

Peace Corps, 24, 39
Profiles in Courage (Kennedy), 18, 39
PT-109, 12-13, 38

Roosevelt, Franklin, 10
Ruby, Jack, 39

segregation, 27, 32-33
Shepard, Alan, 25, 39
Sirhan, Sirhan Bishara, 36
southern Democrats, 19, 28
Soviet Union, 23-27, 34, 39
space program, 25, 32, 39
Stevenson, Adlai, 18, 39

unemployment insurance, 18-19
United Kingdom, 34

Vietnam, 39

Warren Commission, 37
Why England Slept (Kennedy), 11
World War II, 11-12, 16, 29, 38